C-1. Mirrors by Ethie Williamson. See also figures 3-4 and 3-5. (Photo by Beverly Rush.)

C-2. Girl (with whole-wheat hair) and apple by Sannie Olsborg. See also figure 3-33. (Photo by Beverly Rush.)

C-3. Santa plaque by Susan Adamson. See also figure 5-25. (Photo by Beverly Rush.)

C-4. *Carnival Horse* by Mary Ann Spawn. (Courtesy of the artist. Photo by Beverly Rush.)

C-5. Clown (with frostinglike decorations) by an Ecuadorian artist. See also figure 1-1. (Photo by Beverly Rush.)

C-7. Mirror frame by Ethie Williamson. See also figure
5-42. (Photo by Beverly Rush.)

C-6. Ornaments by K Morgan. See also figure 3-16.
(Photo by Beverly Rush.)

C-8. Detail of figure C-7. (Photo by Beverly Rush.)

C-9. *Contemporary American Flag* by Roby's group, Captain Wilkes fifth-grade class. See also figures 8-1, 8-2, 8-3, and 8-4. (Photo by Garnie Quitslund.)

C-10. Christmas trees. (Photo by Garnie Quitslund.)

C-11. Cutout ornaments by Susan Petelik. See also figure 3-2. (Photo by Garnie Quitslund.)

C-12. Figures by Sannie Olsborg. See also figure 3-9. (Photo by Beverly Rush.)

C-14. Ornaments by Ethie Williamson. (Photo by Garnie Quitslund.)

C-13. Back and front of dyed-clay figure by Cherry Valley Enterprises. (Photo by Garnie Quitslund.)

C-15. Mirror frame by Nancy Riddle. An orange-shellac coating colors the natural clay. See also figures 4-15 and 4-16. (Photo by Garnie Quitslund.)

C-16. Mask by Kathy Eyler. See also figures 5-3 and 5-4. (Photo by Garnie Quitslund.)

C-17. *Balthazar* by Cherry Valley Enterprises. (Photo by Beverly Rush.)

C-18. Dyed-clay figure by Susan Adamson. See also figure 4-10. (Photo by Beverly Rush.)

C-19. Mask painted with high-gloss enamels by Robert Lucas. See also figures 6-6 and 6-7. (Photo by Beverly Rush.)

C-20. *Chief's Hat* by Kathy Eyler. See also figure 5-9. (Photo by Beverly Rush.)

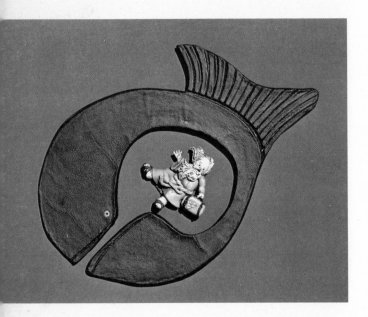

C-21. *Jonah and the Whale* by Ethie Williamson. See also figures 5-34 and 5-35. (Photo by Beverly Rush.)

C-22. Detail of Victorian house by Ethie Williamson. See also figures 5-45 and 5-46. (Photo by Beverly Rush.)

C-23. *Goldilocks and the Three Bears* by Ethie Williamson. See also figure 4-32. (photo by Beverly Rush.)

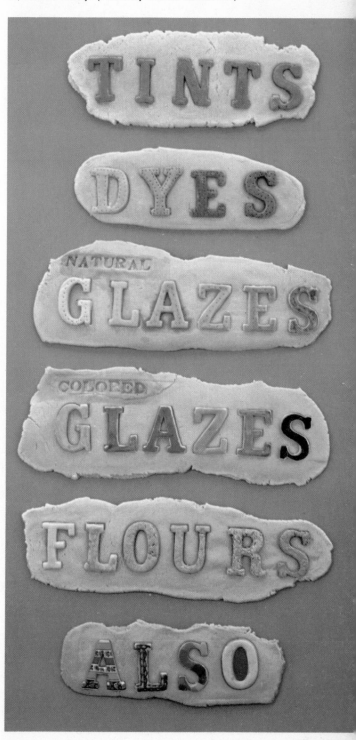

C-24. A variety of color and textural effects is available by these means: T, curry; I, cinnamon; N, paprika; T, black pepper; S, instant coffee; D, food coloring; Y, writing ink; E, tempera; S, fabric dye; G, natural clay; L, mayonnaise; A, egg white; Z, egg white and yolk mixed; E, egg yolk; S, canned milk; G, food coloring; L. coffee; A, tempera; Z, egg yolk; E, writing ink; S, fabric dye; F, white; L, white mixed with cereal grains; O, whole wheat mixed with cereal grains; U, whole wheat; R, rye; S. bran; A, glued fabric; L. dyed-clay frosting; S, color crayon; O, melted candy. (Photo by Garnie Quitslund.)

C-25. Egg yolk tinted with coffee glazed the sun's face; mayonnaise glazed the braided frame. See also figure 5-26. Plaque by Susan Adamson. (Photo by Beverly Rush.)

C-26. Dyed-clay clock by Loch Adamson and Cairn Adamson. See also figures 5-28 and 5-29. (Photo by Beverly Rush.)

C-28. Crushed-candy butterfly by Ethie Williamson. See also figure 6-8. (Photo by Garnie Quitslund.)

C-27. *Purple Sea Urchin Basket* by Kathy Eyler. The light-brown areas were made with whole-wheat flour. Coffee was used to dye the dark-brown clay. See also figure 5-11. (Photo by Beverly Rush.)

baker's clay

baker's clay

cutouts, sculptures, and projects with flour, salt, and water

Ethie Williamson

VNR **VAN NOSTRAND REINHOLD COMPANY**
New York Cincinnati Toronto London Melbourne

Dedicated to Ron, Jennifer, David, and Emily
with special thanks to Bev, Eve, Joanne, Joe, and Lillian

Frontispiece. Pieces of colored clay were added to the
basic Santa cutouts by Susan Adamson and Cairn
Adamson (at age 7). A 4½" cookie cutter was used.
(Courtesy of the artists. Photo by Garnie Quitslund.)

Copyright © 1976 by Litton Educational Publishing, Inc.
Library of Congress Catalog Card Number 76-4449
ISBN 0-442-29487-5   (cloth)
ISBN 0-442-29486-7   (paper)

Printed in the United States of America
Designed by Loudan Enterprises

Published in 1976 by Van Nostrand Reinhold Company
A Division of Litton Educational Publishing, Inc.
450 West 33rd Street
New York, NY 10001

Van Nostrand Reinhold Limited
1410 Birchmount Road
Scarborough, Ontario M1P 2E7, Canada

Van Nostrand Reinhold Australia Pty. Ltd.
17 Queen Street
Mitcham, Victoria 3132, Australia

Van Nostrand Reinhold Company Ltd.
Molly Millars Lane
Wokingham, Berkshire, England

16 15 14 13 12 11 10 9 8 7 6 5 4 3

Library of Congress Cataloging in Publication Data

Williamson, Ethie.
  Baker's clay.

  Includes index.
  1. Bread dough craft. I. Title.
TT880.W54   745.5   76-4449
ISBN 0-442-29487-5
ISBN 0-442-29486-7 pbk.

Contents

Introduction   7

1. History of Decorative Bread Making   9

2. How to Begin   11

3. Small Cutouts   13

4. Small Formed Objects   34

5. Large Projects   55

6. Decorative Treatments   80

7. Preserving Your Work   88

8. Teaching Baker's Clay to Groups   90

Index   94

Introduction

Baker's Clay (by Cairn Adamson, age 11)
Bread dough and baker's clay
One for tomorrow, the other today.
Every shape changing, like passing thoughts;
Pinch it, poke it, and press it in spots.
And with the deciding and debating
Comes the satisfaction of creating.

Baker's clay is a happy medium that makes the joy of creating easily accessible to everyone. It gives all the delight a child gains from mud pies, all the pleasure an artist gains from sculpture. Handling the clay seems to come instinctively—the most inexperienced amateur can create fun works of art that have cookie-like appeal; serious craftsmen enjoy the clay's versatility, its wonderful response to imagination and skill.

Baker's clay is low in cost and easily accessible, and no special studio space is needed. Any flat, smooth surface can be a work area, so the entire family can get involved anywhere at any time. If your children are climbing the walls, mix them up a batch and ask if you can share. The tactile quality of the clay makes it relaxing for both adults and children. (The clay doesn't taste good and is nontoxic, making it an excellent medium for young children.)

Baker's clay is a wonderful, joyous happening and everyone's invited!

I-1. Bread and baker's clay. (Photo by Garnie Quitslund.)

1-1. Ecuadorian clown (7″ × 13½″) with frostinglike
decorations, baked for All Souls' Day. (Photo by Beverly
Rush.)

1. History of Decorative Bread Making

The history of baker's clay is the history of decorative bread making. The first evidence of bread making itself was found in the remains of the Swiss Lake Dwellers, who lived 10,000 years ago. By the time the Egyptian civilization started to develop 5,000 years later, the discovery that bread dough could be manipulated into shapes had been made. The celebration of baker's clay began.

The raising of grains converted some of the herd-following primitive people into stationary farmers. Communities started to develop and grew into towns. They organized to protect themselves against wandering tribes and formed governments. If the harvest was good, they celebrated; if the grain crop failed, so did the community. Bread became an intricate part of religious ritual, and fancy breads were prepared for special occasions. The first cookies (a form of bread) symbolized animals. They probably served as token sacrifices to the gods.

The Egyptians refined different kinds of flour (including wheat), discovered yeast (as did the Chinese), and baked in ovens to produce bread much the same as we know it today. They molded bread into many shapes—fish, birds, pyramids—either by hand or in elaborate bread molds. Bakers competed with each other to produce the fanciest loaves for religious offerings.

The Egyptians' knowledge of bread making was adopted and refined by the Greeks and Romans, who held bread sacred and sacrificed images made of bread to their gods. They also molded bread into fanciful shapes of mushrooms, birds, and lyres. The Romans improved the cultivation of wheat and introduced their knowledge of flour and bread making into what is now Europe.

With the coming of Christianity bread was no longer baked for pagan gods, but it remained an intricate part of religion. Eating bread during Holy Communion symbolized the ingestion of Christ's body. Ornamental breads were baked for feasts on Christmas, Easter, and other church holidays. Each area had its own specialty that is still traditional today—English hot-cross buns at Easter and German stollen (which represents the Christ Child in swaddling clothes) at Christmas, for example.

Other shapes were developed for other occasions. In Hamlin of Pied Piper fame bread is formed in the shape of miniature rats. Crescent rolls (a Mohammedan symbol) were first made in Vienna to celebrate the repulsion of the Turks.

In the Middle Ages bread became functional as well as decorative and edible. Platters made from dough, or trenchers, were placed under the meat to sop up all the drippings. After the diners had cleaned their plate, they ate the trenchers.

In the 16th through the 18th centuries gingerbread was molded into fancy shapes and given as gifts. At the birth of Peter the Great 120 loaves of gingerbread were given to the Czar, two of them weighing 100 pounds each. One represented the Imperial double eagle, and the other reproduced the Kremlin—horse-men surrounded the buildings, and the scene was adorned with dozens of birds and animals.

The only trouble with bread as an artistic medium is its impermanence (there's always someone or something around who will take a bite). Inedible forms of bread began to appear in parts of Europe and South America, the most famous being Ecuadorian bread-dough figures. These figures, originally designed to celebrate All Souls' Day, are now found on many North American Christmas trees.

The first use of baker's clay in North America was in schoolrooms. Everyone past the age of 50 seems to remember turning dough into a relief map! Today, because of its versatility, low cost, accessibility, and non-toxicity, baker's clay has become a favorite of craftsmen, hobbyists, families, invalids, children's groups, and clubs with bazaars. Baker's-clay items are good sellers. They are appealing, and prices can be low because so little expense is involved. Baker's clay can be used to make great home decorations for special occasions, and because it is so easy to work with, it is a good therapeutic activity for the handicapped and just plain fun for school classes, projects, and clubs of all kinds.

2. How to Begin

Baker's clay consists of flour, salt, and water. When the proper quantities of each are mixed together, a claylike dough is produced. It can be flattened, cut, rolled, pinched, coiled, braided, layered, squeezed through a garlic press, or pressed into a mold. You can stick things in it, stamp things on it, and poke holes through it. When the clay is baked, it is extremely hard, similar to ceramic clay. At varying oven temperatures all kinds of materials may be baked in, on, under, or through the raw dough. In comparison to similar mediums, baker's clay is fast. As soon as a shape is formed, it can be baked—no waiting time is necessary. It is also very flexible—it can be baked, additional clay added, and rebaked at the same oven temperature. Or if it's time to fix dinner and the oven is full of baker's clay, just pull it out and return it to the oven at your convenience. With proper protection and care baker's-clay projects will last for an indefinite period of time.

Here are two recipes for baker's clay:

Claylike Mix
2 cups flour
1 scant cup table salt
¾ cup water*
1 ounce glycerine (optional)

Doughlike Mix
4 cups flour
1 cup table salt
1½ cups water*
2 ounces glycerine (optional)

The first resembles ceramic clay, while the second is more like dough. The author prefers the claylike mix, but the other is more widely used. Try both recipes to see which one you like.

Glycerine is expensive and unnecessary for most projects. Glycerine lubricates the dough so that it can be stretched and expanded more easily. This "stretchability" is helpful in rolling out the dough and necessary in making long coils (over 10"). If you use glycerine, compensate by reducing the amount of water.

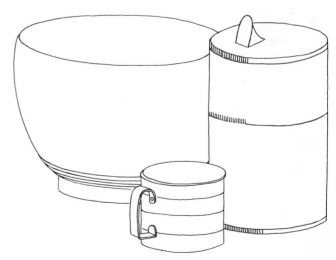

2-1. Baker's-clay ingredients.

*Flour and salt absorb moisture from the air. The amount of water to use depends on the humidity of the area.

11

To make up either of the recipes, follow these instructions.

1. Measure the flour and salt into a medium-size mixing bowl. Stir until the ingredients are well blended.

2. Add the water, mixing as you pour. Add more flour or water as needed. Keep the mix slightly dry if you are adding liquid color. The clay should be soft and smooth, yet stiff enough to hold its shape.

3. Turn the clay out on a lightly floured board. Knead 5 to 10 minutes—until you've worked out your frustrations. The more frustrations, the more pliable the clay! When you knead the mix, the gluten in the flour develops into long, elastic strands.

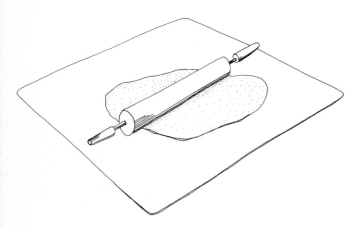

2-2. Roll out the dough.

Here's how to roll out the clay.

1. Flour the rolling pin and the roll-out area generously.

2. Shape the clay into a flattened mound on the floured surface. Flip it over to coat both sides with flour.

3. Roll out to the desired thickness, occasionally flipping over. See the individual projects for precise measurements—the average thickness for a cutout is ¼". Roll the clay paper-thin to assimilate additions such as fabric for a formed figure.

4. Check both sides of the clay to see which has the better surface. Invert if the bottom is smoother.

5. Don't expose the clay to the air for any length of time. Cover the portion to be used with waxed paper.

Baker's clay is baked in the oven. The temperature and time depend on the thickness of the design and the materials added. See the instructions for individual projects. For convenience most projects are constructed on the back of a cookie sheet.

The average baking time for formed objects is 1 hour at 350°. Rolled-out objects bake at 150° for about 8 hours—you can do it while you sleep. These items have a tendency to puff during baking: a low oven temperature usually eliminates the problem.

Bake until the clay is completely firm: poke the front and back with a toothpick to make sure. If a piece sticks to the cookie sheet, it has probably not cooked enough.

Baker's clay becomes stronger during baking. It also expands, fusing the individual parts. Air drying is not usually advisable, although pieces may be baked for a short time and set out in warm, dry air.

3. Small Cutouts

Cutouts are a good place to begin your baker's-clay celebration. Roll out the clay until it is about ¼" thick and either cut out shapes with a cookie cutter, cut around a pattern with a knife, or, if you are adventurous, tear or cut shapes freehand. After you cut out the clay, you can create interesting effects by distorting the shape: flatten it with a rolling pin, twist it around, or overlap areas. Animate a cutout figure by bending its arms, legs, and head; prop them up with wadded aluminum foil to bake the shapes into position.

Texture and color may be added to the rolled-out clay. Imprint the clay with various kitchen gadgets, or, for subtle changes in texture, combine clay with different types of flour as described in chapter 6. Color can be kneaded into the clay, applied after baking, or created by layering different-colored clays before cutting to make fantastic color patterns. Coloring techniques are described in chapter 6; layering, later in this chapter.

No matter how you cut out the shapes for your project, you will need these materials:
1. flour
2. prepared baker's clay
3. rolling pin
4. plastic pastry sheet or smooth roll-out area
5. paring knife with a smooth cutting edge
6. small bowl of water
7. cookie sheet
8. cookie cutter or pattern (optional)
9. wire or hairpin (optional)

3-1. Variations on a gingerbread-man shape.

3-2. Kids, pigs, and horse by Susan Petelik. The line designs were made with coloring pens. The pig-shaped cookie cutter measures 2½″ × 3″. (Photo by Garnie Quitslund.)

3-3. Barn-sweepings wreath by Judy Thomas. The ribbons are secured by 4″ baker's-clay buttons. (Courtesy of the artist. Photo by Garnie Quitslund.)

Cookie-cutter Cutouts

This project is good for a beginner because it gets you over the hurdle of where to start. It is also the easiest way to mass-produce ornaments, place cards, or party favors. Dozens of gingerbread men are charming on a Christmas tree; if they are made from baker's clay they can be kept for years.

3-5. Detail of figure 3-4. Birds were formed from an hors-d'oeuvre cutter. (Photo by Garnie Quitslund.)

3-4. The frames were made by using graduated-size cookie cutters (average height 4"). (Photo by Beverly Rush.)

Make baker's-clay cookies, giving them your own style by adding to or taking away from the basic cookie-cutter shape. Study the shapes of your cutters. With a little alteration, subtraction, or addition a gingerbread man can be transformed into a clown; a club (playing-card symbol) can become a tree; a doughnut can become a picture frame.

Follow this general procedure for cutout forms.

1. Add a pressed design to the rolled-out clay if desired (see figure 3-25).
2. Flour the cutting edge of the cookie cutter.
3. Press the cutter down firmly through the clay. Wiggle the cutter from side to side to release the shape completely. If you are using a cutter with an intricate design, place the rolled-out clay on the baking sheet, make the cut, and remove the surrounding clay.
4. Transfer the cutout to the baking sheet. Gently reshape the form and smooth the edges.

5. To add additional clay, moisten the areas on which you are building.
6. For a hanging object simply make a hole through the clay, bend a 3″ wire into a "U" shape, or use a hairpin; insert the ends of the wire down through the top of the object, leaving a ¾″ loop exposed.
7. Bake at 150° for about 8 hours.

Freestanding cookie-cutter forms (figure 3-7) may be made in this manner.

1. Make two cuts. Place the shape on the back of a cookie sheet.
2. Bend the standing area slightly and prop it up with wadded aluminum foil before and during baking. Bake at 150° until the clay is hard to the touch.
3. Glue the two sections together or add more clay at the contact points and rebake.

3-6. Frostinglike decorations on an Ecuadorian piece transform a basic star into a smiling 4″-wide sun with its tongue sticking out. (Photo by Garnie Quitslund.)

16

3-7. Clown (6" high) by David Williamson (age 10). Free-standing cookie-cutter project. (Photo by Garnie Quitslund.)

3-8. Clowns made from a 5¾"-tall cookie cutter. One figure was turned over so that the two would face each other. (Photo by Garnie Quitslund.)

Pattern Cutouts

You may feel more secure if you plan your design on paper, and a pattern has the advantage of being reusable. Start with flat, simple shapes—coloring books, fabric, and wallpaper are good sources for designs. A pattern enables you to cut out individual sections separately and join them after baking. This procedure is used for designs with movable parts and for some freestanding objects. See chapter 5 for projects larger than 10".

Sections of figures 3-11 and 3-12 are movable. Before baking such a piece, make holes in the raw dough corresponding to the movable parts and join the sections loosely with string after baking. In figure 3-11 the string hanger joins the two sections, and the knots of the string form the eyes.

3-9. Pattern-cut dancing ladies (average height 7") by Sannie Olsborg. (Courtesy of the artist. Photo by Beverly Rush.)

3-10. *Bamse and Friends* by Sannie Olsborg (height of bear 6"). (Pattern cut courtesy of the artist. Photo by Garnie Quitslund.)

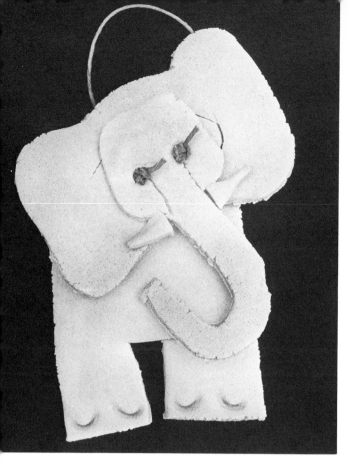

3-11. Pattern-cut elephant (height 5″) with movable head by Mary Ellen Gorham. (Photo by Beverly Rush.)

3-12. Pattern-cut frog (height 5″) with movable legs by Mary Ellen Gorham. (Photo by Beverly Rush.)

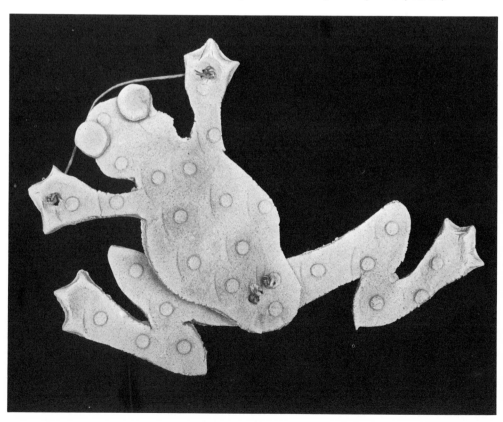

The arms and legs of the doll shown in figure 3-13 illustrate another method to attach movable parts.

1. Push wires into the raw dough.
2. Make a hole in the tops of the movable sections.
3. After baking string the wire through the sections.
4. Crimp the ends of the wire to hold them loosely.

Freestanding objects can be made with a pattern in the same way as with a cookie cutter, or the sections can be slotted before baking and joined afterwards (figure 3-14). To shape the curved body, support the curves with wadded aluminum foil before and during baking.

Here is the general procedure for pattern cutouts.

1. Transfer your design to a piece of heavy paper—recipe file cards are a good weight—and cut out the design.
2. Add a pressed design to the clay if desired (figure 3-36).
3. Place the pattern on the baker's clay and cut around the pattern with a knife, using a sawing motion.
4. Remove the surrounding clay.
5. Place the cutout on the back of a cookie sheet, smooth the edges, and insert a hanger or make a hole.
6. Bake at 150° for about 8 hours or until the clay is hard to the touch.

3-13. Pattern-cut baker's-clay *Penny Doll* (height 5″) by Mary Ann Farmer. (Photo by Garnie Quitslund.)

3-14. *Nessy* (12″ long) by Jennifer Williamson (age 11), done in the freestanding-pattern procedure. The curving body was made by draping and baking the clay over mounds of aluminum foil. (Photo by Garnie Quitslund.)

Freehand Cutouts

Patterns and cookie cutters do limit your creativity—it's time to loosen up and give yourself and the baker's clay a feeling of spontaneity. Use the irregular, natural edges of the rolled-out clay or tear or cut the shapes freehand. Follow the same general procedure as for pattern or cookie-cutter cutouts.

3-15. A free-cut-design pig (3″ long) by Cherry Valley Enterprises. The pig is mounted on fabric. (Photo by Beverly Rush.)

3-16. Free-cut-design bird (4″ high) by K Morgan. (Courtesy of the artist. Photo by Beverly Rush.)

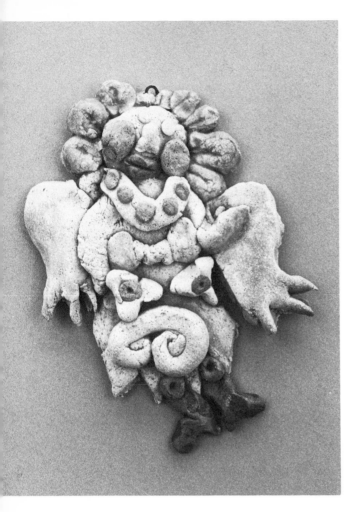

3-17. Free-cut-design angel (7½″ high) by Cairn Adamson (at age 9). (Courtesy of the artist. Photo by Garnie Quitslund.)

3-18. Weed plaque (4½″ × 9″) made from pieces of torn clay in contrasting-colored flours. Pockets were made by draping and baking the clay over coils of aluminum foil. (Photo by Garnie Quitslund.)

Variations

It is easy to add individual touches such as stripes, layers, textures, or imprints to a basic cutout design. Stripes, checkerboards, plaids, swirls, and pinwheels can be made by either stripping or layering clays of assorted colors. Methods of coloring clay are explained in chapter 6.

The procedure for stripping is as follows.

1. Roll out contrasting colors of clay. The clay should be about ¼″ thick.
2. Cut a base from one color of the rolled-out clay. Set it on a cookie sheet and cover with waxed paper.
3. Using a ruler and a knife, cut out strips. Cut a long strip to go around the outside of the design.
4. Moisten the base and attach the strips.
5. Cut out your design (figure 3-20).
6. Add the outside strip (figure 3-21).
7. Add a hanger if desired.
8. Bake at 150° for about 8 hours or until hard.

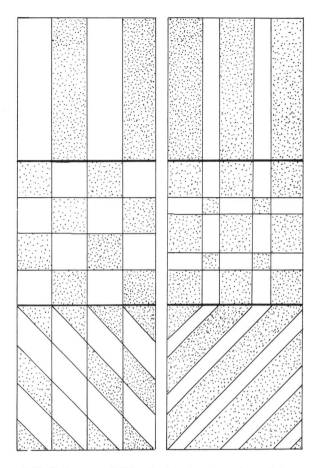

3-19. Pattern possibilities in stripping two colors of clay.

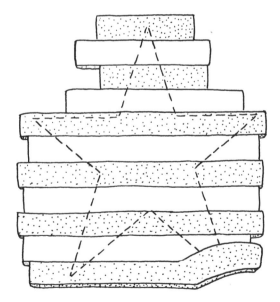

3-20. Joining the stripes.

3-21. Protective strip.

To mass-produce different-colored objects, layer large sections of colored clays. For diversity of line roll the clay out to different thicknesses or fold different layers around each other. Here's how to layer the clay.

1. Roll out the colored clays.

2. Cut the layers to the desired measurements. They may vary in thickness but otherwise should have the same dimensions.

3. Moisten the surface of the bottom section and add the next layer. Gently roll the rolling pin over the layers. Repeat until the desired height is obtained. Don't moisten the top layer unless you are folding the clays.

4. Roll or fold the clays if desired (figures 3-22, 3-23, and 3-24).

5. Use a gentle sawing motion (an electric knife is great!) to slice the clay into ¼" sections. Reshape the clay.

6. Cut out a base and attach your design, as in steps (2) and (4) of the stripping procedure (figure 3-25). Add a strip around the outside of the shape, as in stripping step (6). You can distort the design by rolling the pin over the sliced sections before or after cutting.

7. Add a hanger if desired.

8. Set on a cookie sheet and bake at 150° until hard.

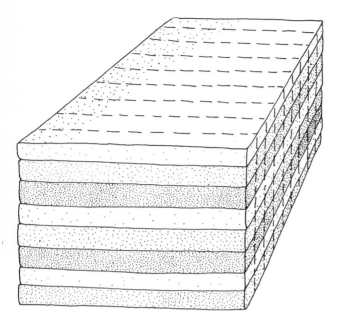

3-22. Layering clay.

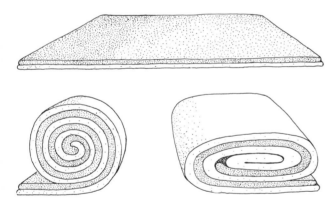

3-23. Roll and fold the layered clay.

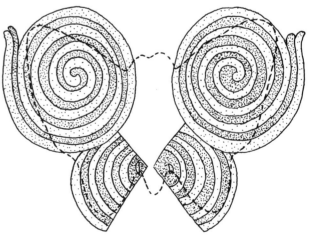

3-24. Arrange the rolled clay for cutout.

3-25. Butterfly made from a 3″-wide cookie cutter and
layered, rolled clay. (Photo by Garnie Quitslund.)

Try a project using an entire section of the rolled-out clay (figures 3-26 and 3-27). Figures 3-28, 3-29, 3-30, and 3-31 show how to make the frame.

3-26. Picture frame (14" in diameter) by Ethie Williamson. Three colors of clay were layered, folded, sliced, and spread, exposing the pattern. The dark polka-dot interior is a thin layer of rolled-out clay. The dots were cut with a plastic drinking straw and replaced with light-colored clay. (Photo by Garnie Quitslund.)

3-27. Detail of figure 3-26. The light- and medium-colored clays were tinted with coffee. The dark clay was dyed with coffee and black food coloring. (Photo by Garnie Quitslund.)

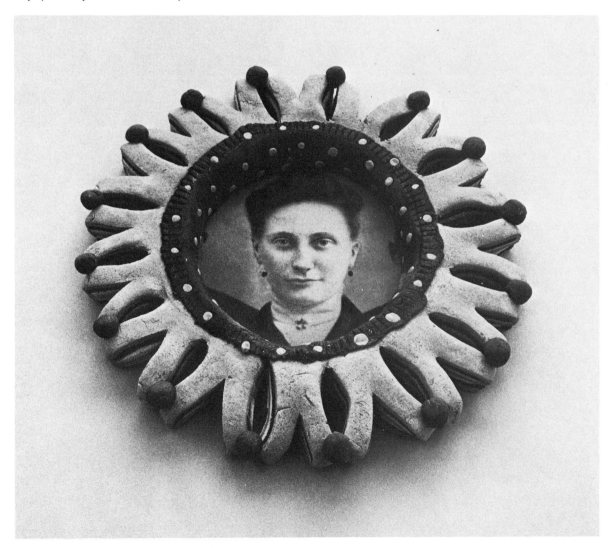

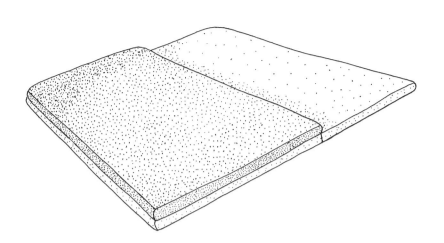

3-28. Roll the outer clay to the desired size—the frame in figure 3-26 measures 12″ × 14″. Roll the inner clay or layers of clay to two-thirds the width of the outer piece—8″ for the 12″ frame.

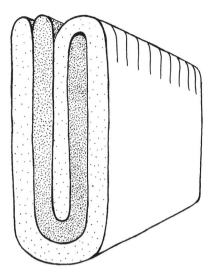

3-29. Layer the clay and fold.

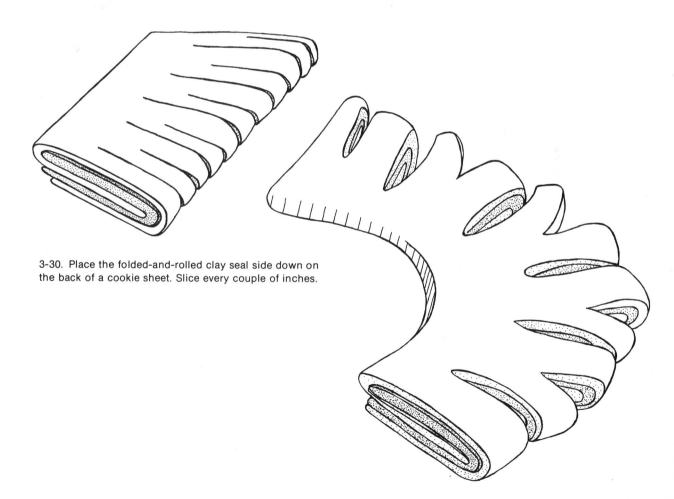

3-30. Place the folded-and-rolled clay seal side down on the back of a cookie sheet. Slice every couple of inches.

3-31. Spread the shape into a circle, semicircle, or oval to expose the color pattern.

The flat expanse of rolled-out clay lends itself to variations in texture. Textural variation can be achieved by joining batches of clay that have been squeezed through a garlic press (figure 3-32) or a potato ricer, by combining batches of clay made with different types of flour (see chapter 6), by adding different materials such as bits of metal to the clay, or by imprinting the surface of the clay with various objects. Anything with a raised or open design can be used to imprint the clay. Textured rolling pins, expanded metal laths, window screening, or chicken wire will cover and texture large surface areas. Smaller objects that will make an interesting pressed design can be found in the utensil, tool, and catchall drawers, in your jewelry and button boxes, and in the children's toy chest. Try meat-grinder gears, buttons, a mallet meat tenderizer, hair rollers, combs, barrettes, hairpins, sieves, snaps, hooks and eyes, a pastry-edge crimper, nails, screws, bolts, nuts, shells, bottlecaps, potato mashers, fork tines, graters, doilies, cut glass, type from children's printing sets—the possibilities are endless. Imprinting the clay will expand the surface slightly, so add the design before you make the cut unless the distortion is desirable.

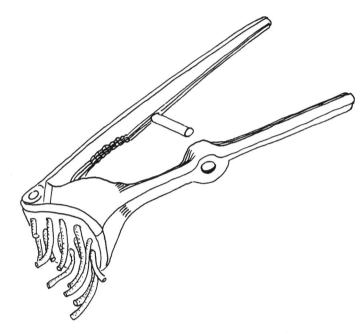

3-32. Baker's clay squeezed through a garlic press.

3-33. Girl with whole-wheat hair by Sannie Olsborg. (Courtesy of the artist. Photo by Garnie Quitslund.)

3-34. Textures created by imprinting the clay with odds
and ends found around the house. (Photo by Garnie
Quitslund.)

3-35. Flower (5½″ × 7″) by Cairn Adamson (at age 6).
A textured, free-cut design. (Courtesy of the artist.
Photo by Garnie Quitslund.)

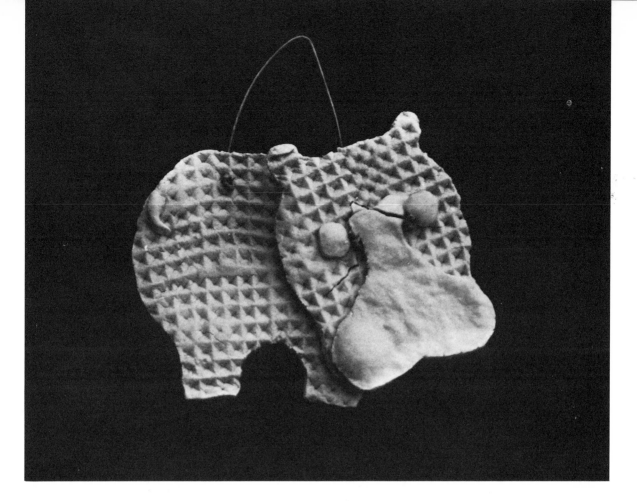

3-36. Baker's-clay hippo (5″ tall), textured with a meat mallet, by Mary Ellen Gorham. (Photo by John Gorham.)

3-37. Textured owl (5″ high) by Mary Ellen Gorham. (Photo by John Gorham.)

Rolled baker's clay can also be shaped and imprinted by pressing it into a mold. Both wooden pastry molds and metal candy molds may be used (figures 3-38 and 3-39), or try the small plastic molds for resins and candles. Coat the surface of the mold to prevent sticking. Use cooking oil on wooden molds; a thin coat of flour or cornstarch, on metal and plastic. Roll the clay out to the desired thickness, making sure that the surface is large enough to cover the shape. Starting with the center of the design and working out, press your fingers into the clay, forcing the air out and the clay into all crannies. Flatten the back of the clay with a rolling pin or knife. Gently peel the clay from the mold, reshape, and trim the edges if desired. Insert the hanger and bake at 150° until the clay is hard to the touch.

3-38. Figures were made by pressing rolled-out clay into lollipop and chocolate candy molds and a wooden cookie mold. (Photo by Garnie Quitslund.)

3-39. A wooden mold formed and imprinted this baker's-clay deer (6″ × 6″) by Mary Ellen Gorham. (Photo by John Gorham.)

4. Small Formed Objects

Hold a piece of baker's clay in your hands. Pinch it, poke it, roll it into a ball. Formed objects are made by combining balls, disks, and coils formed by manipulating the clay in your hands. Keep the clay ball, disk, or coil under 1″ thick—a thicker shape will crack during baking. Figures 4-1, 4-2, 4-3, and 4-4 show how to make these shapes. To unify and smooth the clay, start each formed shape as a ball.

To make a formed object, you will need these materials:
1. baker's clay
2. cookie sheet
3. small bowl of water
4. rolling pin, plastic sheet or smooth roll-out area, and waxed paper (optional)
5. knife (optional)
6. scissors (optional)
7. assorted tools—toothpicks, garlic press, etc. (optional)
8. wire hanger (optional)

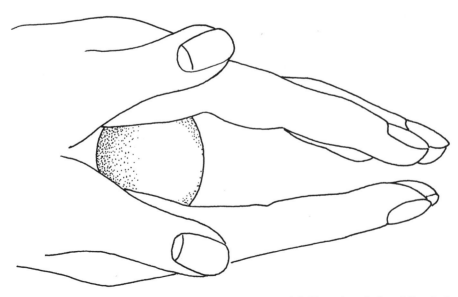

4-1. To make a ball, roll the desired amount of clay in your palms. The movement is like forming an "O" with your hands.

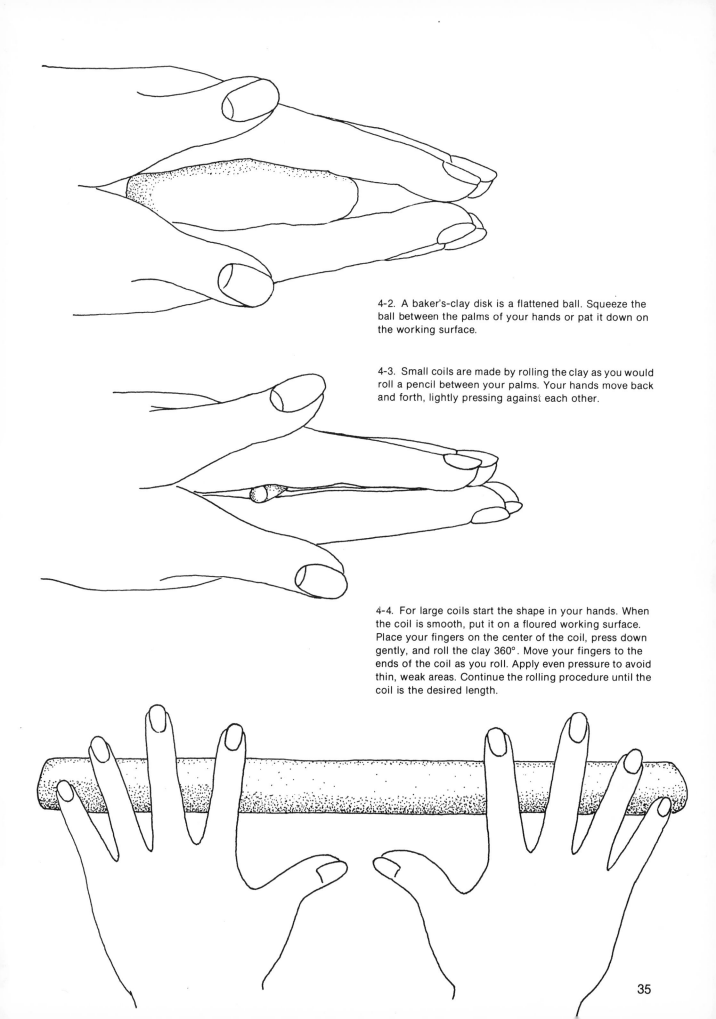

4-2. A baker's-clay disk is a flattened ball. Squeeze the ball between the palms of your hands or pat it down on the working surface.

4-3. Small coils are made by rolling the clay as you would roll a pencil between your palms. Your hands move back and forth, lightly pressing against each other.

4-4. For large coils start the shape in your hands. When the coil is smooth, put it on a floured working surface. Place your fingers on the center of the coil, press down gently, and roll the clay 360°. Move your fingers to the ends of the coil as you roll. Apply even pressure to avoid thin, weak areas. Continue the rolling procedure until the coil is the desired length.

Flat Shapes

Flat shapes are the easiest forms to make. They are the most natural use of the medium—children automatically work this way—and the clay responds readily. They are also the best method for forming layered figures made of different-colored clays.

Here is the basic procedure.
1. Pat out a baker's-clay disk in the palms of your hands or on the working surface.
2. Model the clay disk into the desired shape.
3. Moisten the areas on which you are building and add the other shapes.
4. Add texture or other materials if desired.
5. Attach a hanger if desired.
6. Bake at 200° until the clay is hard. If the clay puffs up, reduce the oven temperature.

4-5. Flat formed clown (6″ high) by Emily Williamson (age 5½). (Courtesy of the artist. Photo by Garnie Quitslund.)

4-6. Flat formed pendant (2½″ × 2¾″) by Laurie Jacobsen (at age 15). (Courtesy of the artist. Photo by Garnie Quitslund.)

4-7. *Smile*, a flat formed wall hanging (6″ in diameter) by Kathy Eyler. (Courtesy of the artist. Photo by Garnie Quitslund.)

4-8. Cats (6¼″ × 6¾) by James K. Morgan. (Courtesy of the artist. Photo by Garnie Quitslund.)

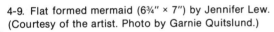
4-9. Flat formed mermaid (6¾″ × 7″) by Jennifer Lew. (Courtesy of the artist. Photo by Garnie Quitslund.)

4-10. Figure (6″ high) by Susan Adamson. The colored-clay sections were rolled flat after forming. (Courtesy of the artist. Photo by Garnie Quitslund.)

4-11. Girl playing the flute (4″ high) by Cherry Valley Enterprises. The flat formed figure was made with dyed clay. (Courtesy of the artist. Photo by Beverly Rush.)

4-12. Flower child with tambourine (4¼″ high) by Cherry Valley Enterprises. Flat formed dyed-clay project. (Courtesy of the artist. Photo by Beverly Rush.)

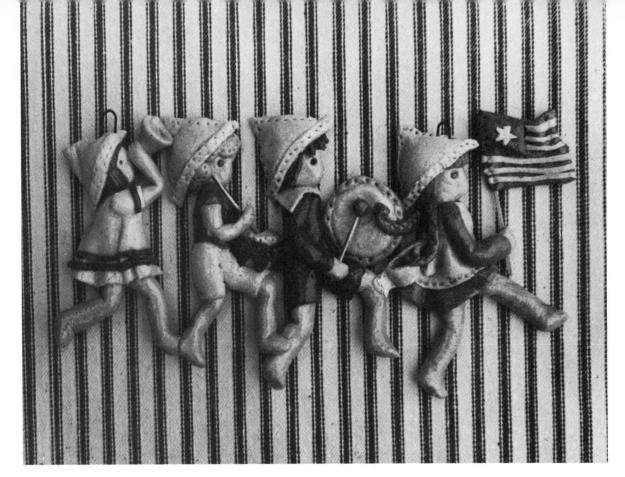

4-13. *Parade* by Cherry Valley Enterprises. A flat formed, dyed-clay project. The flagstaff and drumsticks are toothpicks. (Courtesy of the artist. Photo by Beverly Rush.)

4-14. Kids-in-a-tree plaque (10″ × 13″) by Cherry Valley Enterprises. The swing is wire; the children and the tree are flat formed objects of dyed clay. (Photo by Beverly Rush.)

4-15. Flat formed mirror frame (5″ × 9″) by Nancy Riddle. The baked natural clay was coated with orange shellac. (Courtesy of the artist. Photo by Beverly Rush.)

4-16. Detail of figure 4-15. (Photo by Beverly Rush.)

4-17. Napkin rings by Judy Thomas. Baker's-clay coils were turned into polka-dot snakes. (Photo by Garnie Quitslund.)

4-18. Wreath (8″ in diameter) made from coils of clay
by Mary Ellen Gorham. The bow and birds were cut from
rolled-out clay. (Courtesy of the Weed Lady. Photo by
Beverly Rush.)

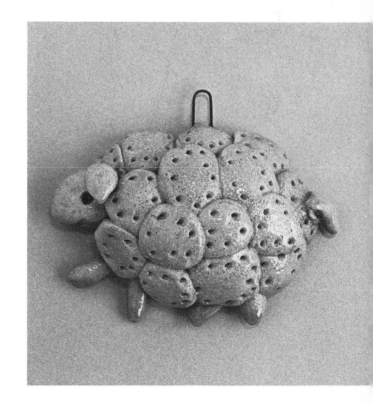

4-19. Sheep (3½″ tall) by Cherry Valley Enterprises.
Small flat disks were added to the formed body and poked
with a toothpick to represent the fleece. (Courtesy of
the artist. Photo by Garnie Quitslund.)

Rounded Shapes

Rounded designs are made by building with and/or on coils and balls. Although the backs of the pieces become flat during construction, the objects invoke a three-dimensional feeling.

Most baker's-clay tree ornaments are small, rounded figures. These joyous, whimsical, cookielike shapes are fun all year round, but they especially seem to personify Christmas. Make some for your tree but keep the figures small—large, heavy items will pull down the branches. Figures 4-20 through 4-28 explain the procedure in detail.

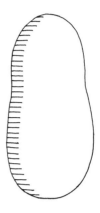

4-20. Place one-quarter of the baker's-clay mix on a heavy plastic sheet or a smooth countertop. Roll the clay paper-thin and cover with a sheet of waxed paper to prevent drying. To make the body, start with a 1″ ball of baker's clay. Roll into a coil 1¼″ × 2½″. Place the coil on the back of a cookie sheet. Shape the body with your fingers.

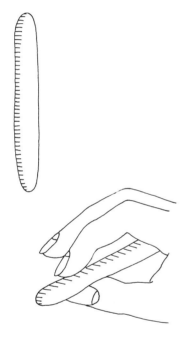

4-21. To make the legs, roll a 1″ ball of clay into a coil 1½″ × 3″. Rotate the coil between your thumb and forefinger ¾″ from the bottom of the leg to create an ankle and heel.

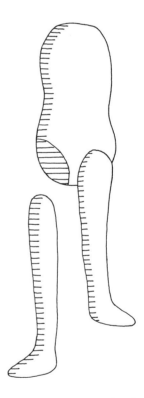

4-22. To make the feet, place your forefinger at the ankle and your thumb a little under the heel; push the foot with your thumb to a 90° angle. Shape the foot and make the indentations for the shoe with a toothpick. Repeat the procedure for the other leg and foot. Moisten the body at the points of contact and attach the legs. Add the clothes you want as described in figures 4-23 and 4-24.

4-23. For a long skirt the section should measure about 4" at the hem, tapering to 2½" at the waist, and 3" long. Moisten the figure at the waist and sides. Place the skirt at the center of the waist and the sides of the skirt at the sides of the legs. At the waist gather the surplus rolled-out clay by making small tucks in the material. Use a toothpick to make the tucks.

4-25. Indent the figure at the shoulders for the arms. To make an arm, roll a ⅝" ball into a coil ⅜" × 2¼". Shape a wrist by rotating the coil between your thumb and forefinger ⅜" from the bottom of the arm. Moisten the shoulder and attach the arm. Repeat the procedure for the other arm.

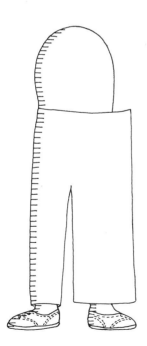

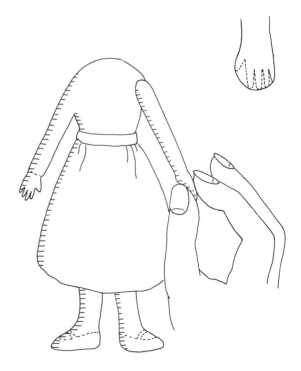

4-24. For pants cut a section 3" × 3". Cut a slit three-quarters up to form the pant legs. Moisten the lower portion of the body and legs. Attach the pants to the body and to both sides of the legs. Cut away excess material with a knife.

4-26. To create a hand; pinch and flatten the area below the figure's wrist. Cut and separate the fingers and thumb with a knife or scissors. Remember to point the thumbs toward the body.

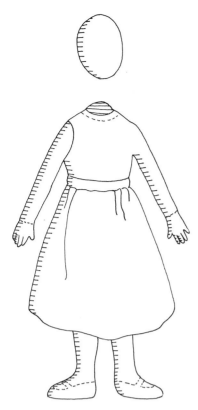

4-27. Cut a collar from the rolled-out clay or score a neckline with a toothpick. A neck is not required, but if you want one, roll a ¼" ball into a coil and attach at the neckline. To make the head, roll a ¾" ball into an egg shape. Indent and moisten the neck area and secure the head to the body.

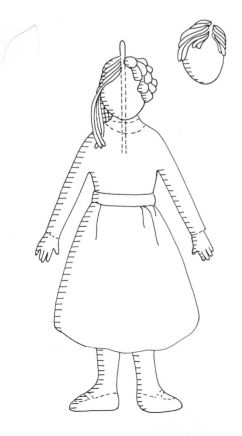

4-29. *Little Miss Muffett* (4" high) by Ethie Williamson. (Courtesy of the Moore family. Photo by Garnie Quitslund.)

4-28. Add features if desired—they can be painted on. All kinds of marvelous hairdos can be made from dough squeezed through a garlic press. The strands can be made into short haircuts, shags, long, straight hair, or pigtails. Curls can be made from small coils of clay. Moisten the head and attach the desired hairstyle. If the figure is to be hung, it will need a hanger. Bend a 3" wire into a "U" shape or use a hairpin. Insert the ends of the wire down through the head and body, leaving a ¾" loop exposed. Check to make sure that the wire does not pierce through the sides of the figure.

4-30. *Red Riding Hood and Wolf* (4″ high) by Ethie Williamson. The wolf's teeth are spaghetti strands. (Courtesy of Jody Nyquist. Photo by Garnie Quitslund.)

4-31. *Humpty Dumpty* before and after (4″ high) by Ethie Williamson. (Courtesy of the Lorenson family. Photo by Garnie Quitslund.)

If you want to display your ornaments all year long but they seem to get lost on the wall, hang them on a wooden découpage plaque (available at art-and-craft shops) or make your own out of baker's clay. Screw cup hooks in the plaque to hang the figures (figure 4-32); they can be transferred to the tree during the holidays. If you want to adhere your figure or design permanently to the plaque, you should build and bake it directly on the wood (figure 4-33). Baker's clay puffs while baking so that the back becomes rounded and curled and does not really fit against a flat surface. When the clay is formed and baked directly on the plaque, however, the materials become one. Children's blocks, barrel lids, or découpage plaques may be used as a base. The wood should be at least ¼″ thick—thinner wood may warp in the oven. Wet the board before applying the clay. Bake at 150° until the thickest part of the design is hard to the touch.

4-32. *Goldilocks and the Three Bears*, plaque (8″ × 9″) by Ethie Williamson. The figures hang from cup hooks that were pushed into the raw-dough house. (Courtesy of the Moore family. Photo by Beverly Rush.)

4-33. Girl with hoop was formed and baked on the backing
of the frame (6½″ × 8″). (Courtesy of the Allen family.
Photo by Garnie Quitslund.)

Sculptures In-the-round

Small baker's-clay items can be built in-the-round if the base is full enough to support the weight. For example, people can be formed in the shape of mounds; animals can be made lying down; snakes and snails can be just crawling along (figure 4-17). Or the clay can be supported with another object, which can either be removed after baking or left in as part of the design. The inside corner of a square cake pan supported the shape of figure 4-36; a miniature tricycle supports figure 4-37. Toothpicks were poked into the body of the figures to support the heads.

The baking temperature and time depend on the prop: the cake pan was baked at 325° for 1 hour; the nutshell and eggshell (figures 4-34 and 4-35) were baked at 150° for about 8 hours. To speed up the baking time, place aluminum foil between the prop and the figure to prevent the materials from fusing. When the clay is partially firm, remove the prop and the foil from the oven. The oven temperature can then be raised, reducing the baking time. Glue the figure to the prop after baking and painting. Figure 4-37 was done in this manner.

4-34. Bunny formed and baked in a duck-egg shell. (Photo by Beverly Rush.)

4-35. Bear in a walnut shell by Nina Gordon. (Photo by Beverly Rush.)

4-36. *Little Jack Horner* (sits 2″ high), small three-dimensional figure by Ethie Williamson. (Photo by Garnie Quitslund.)

4-37. *Giving Bear a Ride*, small three-dimensional figure by Ethie Williamson. (Photo by Garnie Quitslund.)

4-38. The three-dimensional mushrooms (average height 3¼") by Tamsin Mahnken were formed in sections. The unbaked stems were held upright in a raw-dough base. The caps were added after the first baking. (Courtesy of the artist. Photo by Beverly Rush.)

4-39. Mouse's baker's-clay head, arms, and tail were sewn into a cloth body. The figure measures 3″ tall. (Photo by Garnie Quitslund.)

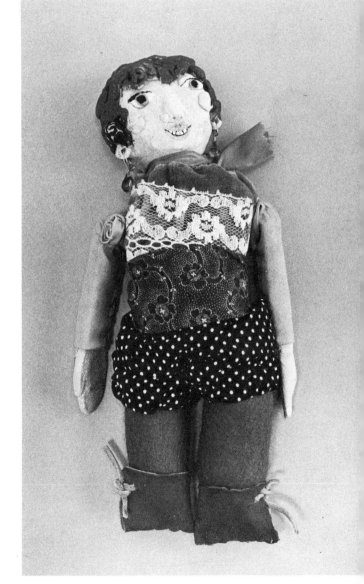

4-40. *French Doll* (7½″ high) by Cairn Adamson (age 11). The pierced earrings were added to the raw-clay head. The body is cloth. (Courtesy of the artist. Photo by Garnie Quitslund.)

5. Large Projects

Three-dimensional Shapes

Large shapes are formed on large objects. Either rolled-out clay or formed coils and disks may be used. As with the smaller items, the supporting object can either be removed or remain as part of the design.

The candleholder in figure 5-5 was constructed over an armature of aluminum foil formed into the basic shape. The rolled-out clay was draped over the foil and molded to it. Figures 5-9 through 5-12 were built over bowls (bottom side up) covered with aluminum foil. Figures 5-3, 5-6, and 5-7 were formed on the back of foil-covered plates.

Woven baskets (figures 5-10 and 5-11), bowls, and dried flowerpots (figure 5-12) can be constructed by interlacing coils or strips of clay. Select a bowl, pan, or pot with the desired shape (no undercuts), invert, and cover with aluminum foil (figure 5-13). Add the vertical strip or coils; starting at the top (bottom of the object), weave the horizontal strips or coils (figure 5-14). If a piece breaks, cut it back to the closest vertical piece and patch it there.

5-2. Detail of figure 5-1. (Photo by Beverly Rush.)

5-1. Baker's-clay plate (10″ in diameter) by Nancy Riddle was formed over an aluminum-foil stoneware plate. (Courtesy of the artist. Photo by Beverly Rush.)

5-3. Baker's-clay mask (4¼″ × 5″) with feathers, bones, and baker's-clay beads by Kathy Eyler. Rolled-out clay was formed over an inverted oval plate covered with aluminum foil. Contrast in color and texture was achieved by using clay made of whole-wheat flour and by mixing the background clay with instant coffee. (Courtesy of the artist. Photo by Garnie Quitslund.)

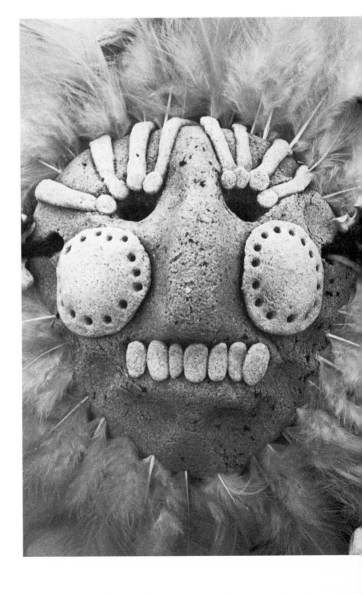

5-4. Detail of figure 5-3. (Photo by Garnie Quitslund.)

5-5. *Lady with Cat* (4″ × 8″), candleholder by K Morgan. Rolled-out clay was draped and molded to an aluminum-foil core. (Courtesy of the artist. Photo by Beverly Rush.)

5-6. Mask (10″ in diameter) by Kathy Eyler. Rolled-out clay was formed over an inverted aluminum-covered plate. (Courtesy of the artist. Photo by Garnie Quitslund.)

5-7. *Scott in the Morning* (9½″ in diameter) by Kathy Eyler. The face was formed over an aluminum-covered plate. Contrasting clays were made from different flours. (Photo by Beverly Rush.)

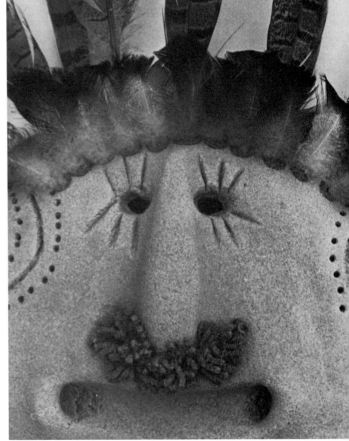

5-8. Closeup of figure 5-6. Pheasant and iridescent wood-duck feathers frame the face. (Photo by Beverly Rush.)

5-9. *Chief's Hat* (6″ in diameter × 17½″ high including feathered top) by Kathy Eyler was built over a bowl. (Courtesy of the artist. Photo by Beverly Rush.)

5-10. Baker's-clay Easter basket (10″ high including handle) by Cherry Valley Enterprises. (Photo by Garnie Quitslund.)

5-11. *Purple Sea Urchin Basket* (9″ × 15″ across the top, 6″ deep) by Kathy Eyler. Flattened coils were added to the outside of a bowl. Handspun Irish yarn, leather, and blackberry-stained sea-urchin shells were added after baking. (Courtesy of the artist. Photo by Beverly Rush.)

5-12. Weed basket (3½" in diameter × 5" high). (Flower arrangement courtesy of Charlotte Mirick. Photo by Garnie Quitslund.)

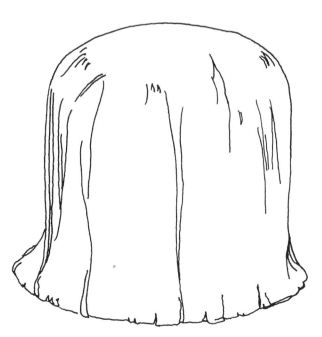

5-13. Cover the bowl with aluminum foil.

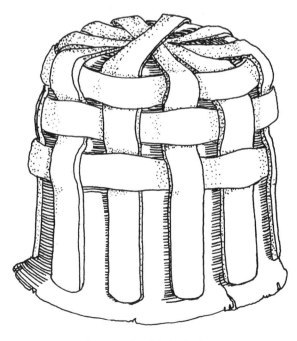

5-14. Weave strips or coils of baker's clay.

5-15. Hanging lamp (top diameter 6″, bottom diameter 13″, 5″ high) by Ethie Williamson. (Photo by Garnie Quitslund.)

One good idea for a woven basket is to invert and convert it into a lamp (figure 5-15).

To make this project, you will need these materials:
1. three batches of clay mixed with glycerine (see chapter 2)
2. floured rolling pin and roll-out sheet
3. plastic bag to store the clay
4. bowl for base
5. aluminum foil
6. cookie sheet
7. knife
8. small bowl for water
9. equipment for electrical wiring

Here is the procedure for making the lamp.
1. Select a bowl. (The bowl in figure 5-15 measures 5½″ in height and 10½″ in diameter. It has a foot that serves as a brace for the braid.)
2. Cover the outside of the bowl completely with aluminum foil. Invert the bowl on to the back of a cookie sheet.
3. Mix three batches of clay with glycerine added. Leave the clay in a plastic bag for about an hour before rolling it out into long coils.
4. Combine two batches. Roll the clay until it is about ⅜″ thick and large enough to cover the bowl.
5. Drape the clay over the bowl. Pinch folds to take up excess material (figure 5-16). Cut away the excess and place in the plastic bag. Smooth the clay with your hands and the rolling pin.
6. Cut out the design and the hole for the electric wire (figure 5-17). Remove excess clay.
7. Start the pretzel and twist shapes as balls 7″ in diameter; roll into coils 3″ in diameter and 20″ long and form (figures 5-18 and 5-19).

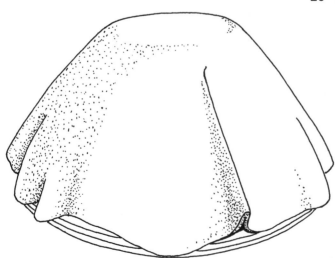

5-16. Drape and pinch the clay to the bowl shape.

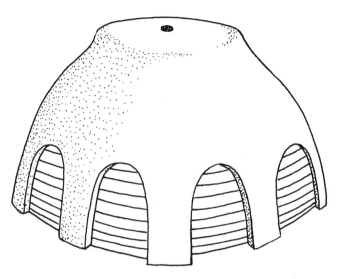

5-17. Cut out the design.

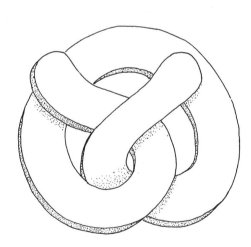

5-18. Form the pretzel shape.

5-19. Form the twist shape.

8. For a better bond make hatch marks on the back of the coils and the area on which you are building. Moisten and add the shapes.

9. Form two coils 2½" in diameter and 20" long. Twist to get a braided effect (figure 5-20). Add the coils to the crest of the bowl and smooth the cut edges.

10. Glaze if desired. (The background area in figure 5-15 was glazed with egg yolk tinted with instant coffee; mayonnaise was applied to the light areas.)

11. Bake at 200° for about 2 hours or until the clay is firm enough to stand by itself. Remove the bowl and return the lamp to the oven.

12. Apply the protective coating (polyurethane). The lamp is fairly heavy (about 5 pounds) and must be supported by a chain or metal tube (figure 5-21). An inverted canopy was placed under the lamp to hold the metal tube and take the weight off the top of the clay.

5-20. Form the braid shape.

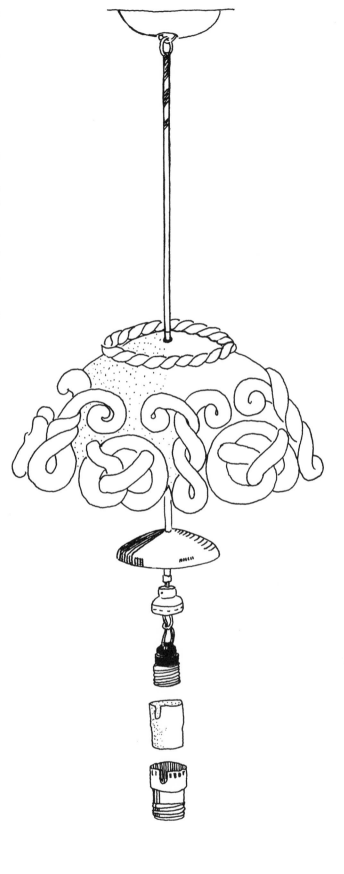

5-21. Wire the lamp.

Plaques and Frames

Baker's clay has no size limitations, but projects over 10″ should be reinforced with another material. A finished clay piece can be glued to a base, or, for a more secure bond (both physically and visually), build and bake the clay on or with the reinforcing material.

Metal and wood can be used as a base; glass and dishwaterproof plastics, in some cases. Glass should be used only if the expansion of the glass and clay is not restricted and if the oven is kept at a low temperature (see chapter 6). Plastics should also be used only at low oven temperatures, and be warned—the smell is overpowering! Wood strengthens the piece as well as giving the clay a workable mounting surface.

If the base is not incorporated in the design, the reinforcing material has to be shaped to fit the pattern. Metal screening or chicken wire can be cut and pushed into the back of raw clay; the clay can also be baked on top of presawn plywood.

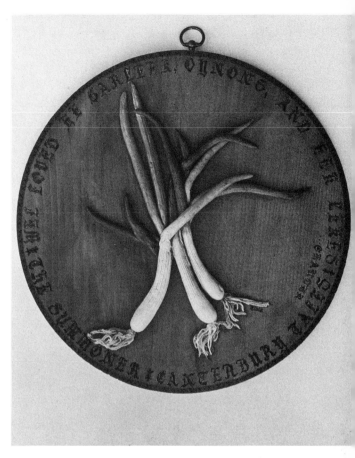

5-22. *Oynons* plaque was formed and baked on a 15″-diameter wooden barrel lid. (Courtesy of the Robins family. Photo by Beverly Rush.)

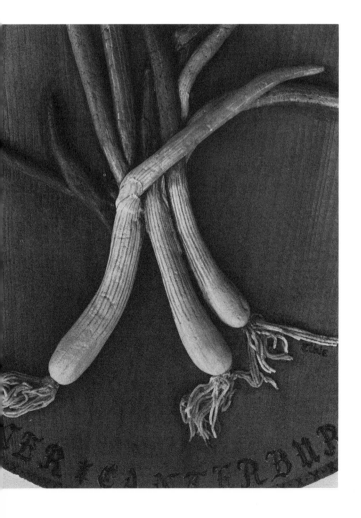

5-23. Detail of figure 5-22. The quotation was burned into the wood with an electric pen from a wood-burning set. (Photo by Beverly Rush.)

The plywood can be cut with a coping saw or an electric saw with narrow blades such as a band, jig, or saber saw (figure 5-24). These types cut curves and corners easily. Don't worry if the surface of the wood is not perfect or if the saw nicks out chunks of wood—the wood will be covered by the clay. Interior cuts are also easily made by running the saw from the outside edge to where the cutout will be. Any cutting lines will be covered by the clay, but if you make a lot of interior cuts, brace the back of the plaque with small strips of wood. After sawing sand the sides to remove splinters.

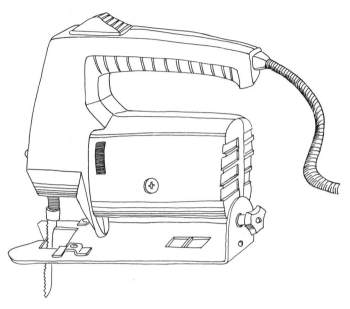

5-24. Saber saw.

5-25. Santa plaque (10″ in diameter) by Susan Adamson. (Courtesy of the artist. Photo by Beverly Rush.)

5-26. Sun plaque (14″ in diameter) by Susan Adamson. Egg yolk glazed the background clay. Mayonnaise was applied to the braided frame. (Courtesy of the artist. Photo by Beverly Rush.)

5-27. Moon plaque (a companion piece to figure 5-26) by Susan Adamson. (Courtesy of the artist. Photo by Beverly Rush.)

5-28. Clock by Loch Adamson (age 7) and Cairn Adamson (age 11). The plywood base was drilled and routed to hold the works of a secondhand clock. (Courtesy of the artists. Photo by Garnie Quitslund.)

5-29. Detail of figure 5-28. The decorations and numerals are dyed pieces of baker's clay. The numbers were cut with cookie cutters purchased from a cake-decorating supplier. (Photo by Garnie Quitslund.)

5-30. Victorian house (12″ × 14½″) by Ethie Williamson. Baker's clay was added to and baked on a wood-and-glass base. The house was braced with strips of wood, permitting light to filter behind the shape. (Courtesy of the Eliason family. Photo by Gabrial Moulin Studios.)

5-31. *Aunt Minnie and Uncle Lathe*, companion pieces by Ethie Williamson. The antique oval frames measure 15½″ × 22″. (Courtesy of the Elliott and Wright families. Photo by Garnie Quitslund.)

5-32. *Graduation 1868* (15″ × 20½″) by Ethie Williamson. The figure and frame are made of baker's clay. The base is layered plywood. (Courtesy of the Plommer family. Photo by Beverly Rush.)

5-33. Detail of figure 5-32. The lace background was added to the raw dough. After painting, antiquing glaze was applied. (Photo by Beverly Rush.)

5-34. *Jonah and the Whale*, plaque (10½″ × 16″) by Ethie
Williamson. (Courtesy of the Lindbergh family. Photo by
Garnie Quitslund.)

5-35. Detail of figure 5-34. (Photo by Garnie Quitslund.)

To make the plaque shown in figures 5-34 and 5-35, you will need these materials:

1. strong lightweight paper (shelf paper), pencil, and transfer paper
2. prepared baker's clay
3. rolling pin and plastic roll-out sheet
4. ¼"-thick plywood
5. saber, jig, band, or coping saw
6. sandpaper
7. white glue (one part water to four parts glue)
8. glue brush or sponge
9. sawtooth mount
10. screw eye
11. grommet
12. knife
13. cookie sheet
14. 4" of fish line

Follow these directions to make the plaque.

1. Work out the design on a piece of lightweight paper.
2. Transfer the design to the plywood.
3. Saw out the design.
4. Sand the edges of the wood.
5. Screw on the mount and screw eye to the back of the wood base (figure 5-36): the pressure of applying a hanger to the finished project might damage the clay. The uneven bottom will make it difficult to add the clay, so prop up the base with wads of aluminum foil. If the mount has to be added after the clay is baked, cushion the project, with the clay face down, on a pillow.
6. Roll out the baker's clay to a ½" thickness. Be sure that the surface is large enough to cover the wood completely.
7. Apply the glue to the entire surface of the wood with a brush or sponge. Use enough glue to make the surface wet and sticky but not so much that it changes the consistency of the clay.
8. Put the clay on top of the wood base.
9. With a rolling pin press and roll the baker's clay onto the wood. At this point the clay should be ⅜" thick.
10. Trim the edges with a knife.
11. Place the paper pattern on top of the baker's clay. With a pencil press down on the lines of the interior design, transferring them to the clay. Remove the paper and score the designs deep into the clay with a knife. For the eye press a grommet deep into the clay (figure 5-37).

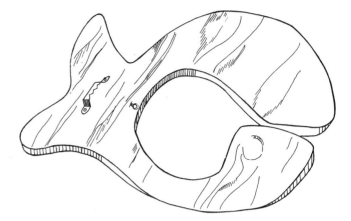

5-36. Add the mount and screw eye to the back of the whale.

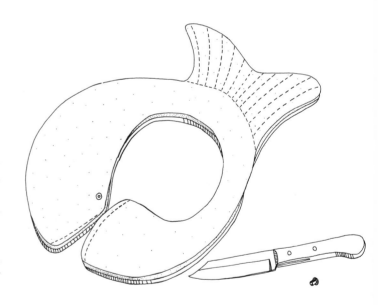

5-37. Press in the details of the whale's mouth and tail; imprint the eye. Bake at 150° for about 8 hours.

12. Bake the plaque at 150° until the fullest section is hard to the touch.

13. Using the plaque as a template, pencil the outline of the stomach on the back of the cookie sheet. Form the figure and suitcase within the stomach line (figure 5-38)—remember that he is in a tumultuous state! Give the figure a feeling of action by swirling the hair and beard and propping up his foot with a wad of aluminum foil. His suitcase is a baker's-clay rectangle; the straps are strips of rolled-out clay.

14. Insert the hanger in the middle of the figure's back (figure 5-39). Bake at 350° for 1 hour.

15. Paint if desired and add protective coating.

16. Attach the fish line to the figure and the plaque.

5-39. Add the hanger to the back of the figure. After baking, painting, and adding a protective coating, attach Jonah to the screw eye with fish line.

5-38. With a pencil score the stomach area on the back of a cookie sheet. Form Jonah and suitcase within the line.

A baker's-clay frame—for a mirror, a picture, or a piece of glass—is a fun way to use the medium. Here again, a wooden base is needed to protect the surface of the object, to give you a flat surface on which to join the object to the frame, and to support the object's weight and take the pressure off the clay. In addition, clay may ruin a mirror's reflectivity. The materials for this project are numbers (1) through (9) in the list for the plaque.

The procedure for the frame is as follows.
1. Transfer your design to the plywood. Be sure that the outside edge of the frame covers the object. The inside dimensions should be smaller than the outside of the object.
2. Saw out the frame. If necessary, nail on strips of wood for bracing.
3. Add the mount. Braces will eliminate any wobbling.
4. Add the clay. Bake at 150° until it is hard to the touch.
5. Paint or stain if desired.
6. Apply a protective coating.
7. Glue the object to the frame.

5-40. Mirror frame (10½" in diameter) by Ethie Williamson. Baker's-clay balls and coils were added to a plywood base. (Photo by Garnie Quitslund.)

5-41. Mirror frame (8" in diameter) made with dyed baker's clay by Cherry Valley Enterprises. (Photo by Garnie Quitslund.)

5-42. Nursery-rhyme mirror (10" in diameter) by Ethie Williamson. (Courtesy of the Moore family. Photo by Garnie Quitslund.)

Projects Larger than your Oven

With a little planning your oven need not limit the size of your design. Large objects can be made in sections and assembled after baking. Figures 5-43 and 5-44 are large sculptures that were formed and baked in sections. Rope joins the sections, holds the pose of the figures, and supports and distributes the weight of the large pieces. Strips of wood 1" × 2" join the sections of figure 5-47. The dress section is Upson board, a type of fiberboard, covered with vinyl oilcloth. The strips also act as braces and extend the shape from the wall so that the spider and the fly can move freely. Instructions are given in figures 5-51, 5-52, and 5-53.

5-43. *Horse and Rider* (54″ × 54″) by Mary Ellen Gorham. Chicken wire was used as a base. (Courtesy of the artist. Photo by John Gorham.)

5-44. *Indian God* (18″ × 18″) by Mary Ellen Gorham. (Courtesy of the artist. Photo by John Gorham.)

5-45. *Victorian House* (19" × 22") by Ethie Williamson. The house was built on three plywood bases. The bases were tiered after baking to give the house more dimension. (Courtesy of the Mahnken family. Photo by Beverly Rush.)

5-46. Detail of figure 5-45. (Photo by Beverly Rush.)

5-47. *There was an Old Lady Who* (18½ × 36"). (Courtesy of the Thorpe family. Photo by Beverly Rush.)

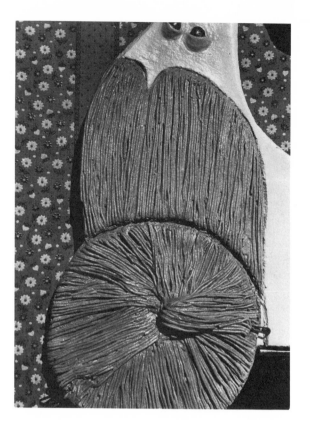

5-48. Detail of figure 5-47. Hairpins were poked into the unbaked garlic-press squeezings. (Photo by Beverly Rush.)

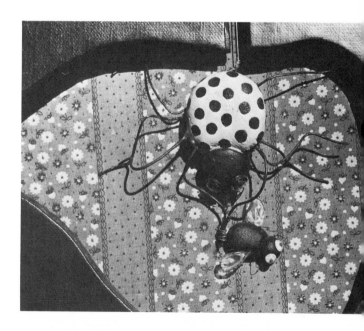

5-49. Detail of figure 5-47. Wires were stuck into the raw dough to represent the legs and wings. The wings were covered with trimmed cellophane tape. The wiggly eyes were glued to the baked form. (Photo by Beverly Rush.)

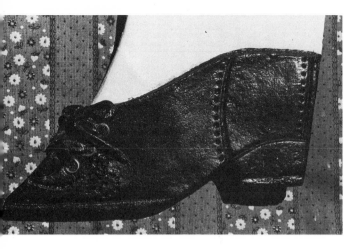

5-50. Detail of figure 5-47. The shoes are a second layer of rolled-out baker's clay. The eyelets are grommets poked into the raw dough. The laces are baker's clay. (Photo by Beverly Rush.)

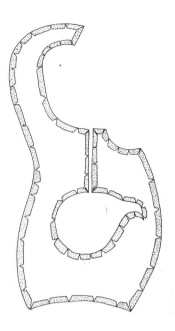

5-52. Vinyl oilcloth was glued and stretched around the Upson board.

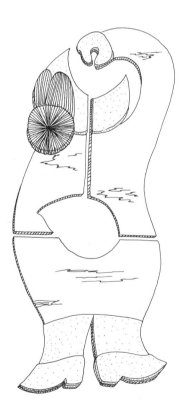

5-51. The figure was cut into workable sections that fit in the oven. Baker's clay was added to legs, shoes, head, hair, and hand area.

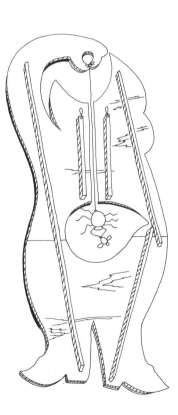

5-53. The sections were joined in the back with 1"-x-2" wood strips. The vinyl-covered board was glued to the front.

6. Decorative Treatments

Tinting, Dyeing, and Glazing

Baker's clay can be glazed, painted, stained, découpaged with fabric or paper, left as is, or colored with natural or commercial dyes. (A tint is a slight coloration, whereas a value change darkens the original color.)

Dyes, whether tints or values, are added to the clay during the kneading process. Baking lightens the color slightly, but most of the intensity returns after treatment with a protective coating. Be careful not to overbake dyed clay: your work will take on a brownish tinge.

If you are working with children, it is very important to keep the clay nontoxic. Dye the clay with food colorings, tempera, or spices. This also applies if you are giving or selling your items.

Some spices will create a subtle change in hue without changing the natural appearance of the clay. Break off the desired amount of clay and knead in the color ingredient. Spices that are good sources of color are mustard, paprika, curry, turmeric, black pepper, cinnamon, and oregano. You can also use instant coffee (see figures 5-3 and 5-4), instant tea, or prepared mustard.

Food coloring, colored inks, and liquid tempera may also be added directly to the dough. Dissolve fabric dyes and dry tempera in water before adding to the mix. These dyes are much stronger and gayer than the natural dyes (see figure 4-14). The paste form of food coloring used by commercial bakers is far more concentrated than the liquid color found at grocery stores. Coloring paste is available at cake-decorating firms, or it can be ordered from their catalogs.

Break off the desired amount of clay; knead in the color. Remember to keep the clay mix a little dry to compensate for the additional moisture. To mix large amounts of colored clay, see chapter 8.

An interesting way to achieve variation in color tone and in texture is to use different types of flour. Substitute whole wheat, rye, bran, buckwheat, or soy flour for white flour in the baker's-clay recipe. These flours are not as elastic as white flour, so the clay will not stretch as easily. Cereal grains can be added to the flour for a more pronounced texture, and rough-milled grains will give the clay more body so that you can build higher shapes. They have a similar effect to adding grog to ceramic clay. Any of these other flours or grains creates a clay with a rough texture that lends itself to natural, homespun, or primitive projects (figure 6-1).

A glaze is a glossy, transparent coating on the surface of the clay. Glazes are applied to the finished form before baking. They can be painted over the entire form or used to accent certain areas.

Canned milk, egg, and mayonnaise are the most commonly used natural glazes. They create variation in value while retaining the natural look of the clay.

Here are some suggestions for natural glazes.

1. Mayonnaise gives the clay a wet, shiny appearance.

2. Egg white beaten with 1 teaspoon of water creates a light-brown glaze.

3. A whole egg beaten with 1 teaspoon of milk gives a shiny, medium-brown glaze.

4. Egg yolk beaten with 1 teaspoon of water gives a yellow-brown glaze.

5. Canned milk produces a dark-brown glaze. For a more pronounced color change additional coats of milk or mayonnaise may be applied during baking. Before adding more egg glaze, however, the clay objects should be cooled.

The best colored glazes are made with egg yolk. Separate the yolk and the white and re-move the membrane of the yolk. Mix the yolk with 1 teaspoon of water. The yolk is the vehicle for adding food coloring, instant coffee or tea, inks, or tempera. Powdered color, instant coffee, and tea should be ground and dissolved in the teaspoon of water before adding to the yolk. Brush the glaze on the finished clay object. Bake at 250° or lower: higher temperatures distort the colors.

You can create a fun glaze with colored crayons. Bake the clay item until it is firm, color, and return to the oven. Continued baking melts and sets the colors.

Although glazes are usually added to an unbaked object, they can be applied to a cool baked form. Brush on the glaze, return the object to the oven, and bake until the color sets.

6-1. *John and Marsha* (8″ × 10″) by Bobbie Quitslund. The variation in value was achieved by using white, whole-wheat, rye, buckwheat, and soy (yellow) flours. (Courtesy of the artist. Photo by Garnie Quitslund.)

6-2. Household objects poked into unbaked clay.

Additions to Unbaked Objects

Many materials can be poked into or layered onto the unbaked clay. The expansion of the clay during baking will hold the materials firmly in place. Pasta, bits of metal, and ceramic objects may be used at oven temperatures up to 350°. Soak pasta in water until it becomes limp to make it flexible. Wood; bone, feathers, pods, shells, and some plastics may be used at lower oven temperatures—up to 200°.

6-3. Mask by Kathy Eyler. Feathers and wires with baked-dough balls and disks were added to the raw-dough head. During baking the wires were held in position with mounds of aluminum foil. (Photo by Garnie Quitslund.)

Do not surround a glass object completely: the expansion of the clay during baking will break it. Glass may also shatter during sudden changes in temperature. Building a clay form over an inverted glass bowl that is placed on a cookie sheet may create a problem, since the temperature inside the bowl will be higher than outside. If you place the object in a cold oven, bake at a low temperature (150°), and allow it to cool before opening the oven, the chance that the glass will break is minimal. Don't add mirrors to unbaked clay: the moisture may ruin the silvering.

By using a plastic pastry tube with assorted tips, frostinglike decorations can be added to the clay (figures 6-4 and 6-5). The "frosting" is moist, old, tired, dyed clay (more than 4 hours old) that has lost its elasticity. Baker's clay on top of baker's clay assures the best bond.

6-4. Mirror frame (10″ in diameter) by Ethie Williamson. The flowers were made by squeezing old, tired baker's clay through a pastry tube with different frosting tips. (Photo by Garnie Quitslund.)

6-5. Detail of figure 6-4. (Photo by Garnie Quitslund.)

Additions to Baked Objects

Paper, fabric, candy, paint—just about anything—can be added to the clay after it is baked. If your project has an open design or if you are making indentations in the clay to hold something such as a mirror, remember that these areas will shrink during baking, so plan your project accordingly.

Use white glue, an acrylic-base découpage product, or polymer emulsion to adhere paper or fabric to baked clay. Seal the finished project with the same product to protect the surface and to keep the fabric or paper from fraying or shredding. Follow the instructions on the container. These coatings will not yellow the fabric or paper.

6-6. Mask (6″ × 8″) by Robert Lucas. The face was pitted with the tip and the eraser end of a pencil. The slash lines were made with a knife. The grasses were laced on after baking. (Courtesy of the artist. Photo by Garnie Quitslund.)

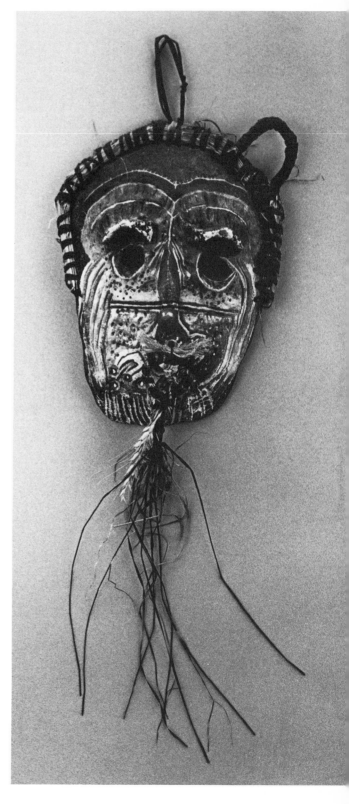

6-7. Detail of figure 6-6. (Photo by Beverly Rush.)

A stained-glass effect can be obtained by adding crushed, colored, transparent candy such as lollipops to the open areas between the clay (figure 6-8). The candy melts during baking, so the bottom of the clay and the baking sheet must be as flat as possible. Place a double layer of waxed paper between the baked clay and the cookie sheet and leave it in during baking. Fill the open areas with the crushed candy and bake at 350° until the candy melts (about 6 minutes). It will lose its color if it is baked too long. Candy projects are fun and dramatic, but they are temporary— the candy melts and drips. Leaving the waxed paper on the back and coating the front with polyurethane helps.

Frostinglike decorations can also be applied to baked clay. Use acrylic-base modeling paste (found at art-supply shops). Squeeze the paste through a cake-decorating tube with assorted tips, a paper cone, or a plastic bag with the corner snipped off (a good technique for children). The paste can be dyed if desired. It takes about 24 hours for the modeling paste and the baker's clay to bond.

Any type of paint may be applied to baker's clay after baking—acrylics, oils, enamels, tempera, or watercolors.

Acrylic colors are permanent, dry rapidly, and are easy to use. They have a plastic base, which makes the paint water-soluble until it dries—then it becomes water-resistant. This protects the clay by keeping the salt from absorbing moisture in the air.

Oil paints have a rich and subtle quality that acrylic paints lack, but they do have their drawbacks. They take a long time to dry; they are oil-based (turpentine must be used to thin the paint and for cleanup); and they do not give the protection of acrylics.

Enamel paints, used for model airplanes, have a hard, protective coating and come in a wide range of colors. They are available at drugstores, variety stores, and hobby shops. Color mixing, however, is a messy operation. Enamels have an oil base, so turpentine must be used for cleanup.

Tempera (poster) paint is inexpensive, so it is usually used by beginners and children. It has a tendency to crack and smear, however, which can frustrate the budding enthusiast. White glue must be added to reduce cracking and smearing. Here are three recipes:

1. one part glue to six parts premixed tempera—good and cheap
2. one part glue to four parts premixed tempera—better but more expensive
3. dry tempera (mixed with a little water to dissolve the granules) and glue—best but most expensive

Egg yolk is a good vehicle for tempera pigments. Remove the egg white and the yolk membrane. Dissolve the paint granules in a small amount of water and mix into the yolk. If you want to keep the tempera for awhile, use distilled water. Cover the unused portion and store in the refrigerator.

You can make an inexpensive acrylic paint by dissolving dry tempera in a small amount of water and mixing it with polymer-emulsion gel (available at art-supply stores).

Watercolors soak into the baker's clay, giving the object a stained effect. They are the best medium for young children, who are inclined to pile on large amounts of paint, thereby losing some of the marvelous detail of their work. Acrylics can be thinned down with water to approximate the transparency of watercolors.

6-8. Butterfly (10″ × 24″) by Ethie Williamson. Crushed
candy was melted in areas that were left open in previously
dyed, baked clay. (Courtesy of the Lorensen family.
Photo by Garnie Quitslund.)

7. Preserving Your Work

There are two things that you have to watch out for with baker's clay: breakage (figure 7-1) and moisture. Unless a piece has shattered completely, most breakage can be repaired. Use a strong glue to mend cracks; missing sections can be patched with new clay and rebaked (figures 7-2 and 7-3). Every precaution must be taken, however, against water and moisture.

Even after the clay is baked, the salt in the mixture absorbs moisture from the air. An unprotected object will swell, become limp, and finally dissolve. A limp, swollen object can be saved by returning it to a warm oven (150°) until it dries out. Here are some other safety measures.

1. Be sure that the object is completely baked or dried.
2. Coat all surfaces with a waterproof seal.
3. Be sure that any hanger is secure and can support the weight of the object.
4. Display or hang an object in a relatively dry area. Do not expose it to any moisture: to steam, in windows, above sinks, or outside.
5. Store seasonal objects in a warm, dry area off the floor. Wrap each piece in tissue and place in a tin with a tight-fitting lid. Plastic bags trap moisture: if the object is not completely dry, it will "sweat" inside the bag.

All baker's-clay objects should be protected with a waterproof seal—varnish, lacquer, shellac, or polyurethane. Orange shellac will produce a pronounced color change—know before you use! The most important aspect of a protective coating is that it must be congenial with the underlying paint. Use an oil-base sealer with oil paint and a plastic-base sealer with acrylic paint. Either type can be used with watercolors, tempera, or glazes. Some sealers will discolor the object. You can use this to your advantage, but test the coating on a small area first before applying it to the whole piece. Most protective coatings come in glossy, semigloss, and mat finishes. Choose the one that best fits your project. A spray coating is usually adequate, but for a more complete seal brush on a liquid coating.

7-1. Broken figure. (Photo by Garnie Quitslund.)

7-2. Figure repaired with white glue and raw baker's clay. (Photo by Garnie Quitslund.)

7-3. Restored figure. (Photo by Garnie Quitslund.)

8. Teaching Baker's Clay to Groups

Baker's clay is an ideal medium for groups of adults or children. It's easy, fun, safe, and inexpensive. Assemble the following tools and materials:

1. flour in bulk
2. salt in bulk (don't use pickling salt—it has a larger grain)
3. water
4. mixing bowls
5. measuring cups
6. plastic drop cloth to place under the working area
7. plastic bags—at least one for each student
8. aluminum foil or baking sheets to model and bake on
9. knives, scissors, rolling pins (make sure that the classroom has a smooth-surfaced area for rolling out the clay)
10. garlic presses and potato ricers—as many as you can get your hands on
11. hairpins or wire and cutters
12. box lids—for students to transport their projects
13. slips of paper with baking instructions and a reminder to remove the cardboard before baking

Ask the adults to bring their own equipment, including a cookie sheet. Show children how to use the equipment, especially the garlic press. They are inclined to overload, which will break the press.

Have the students mix their own clay. This is good training for children, and adults can check the consistency for themselves. Divide the students into groups of two or three. Pro- vide each group with a measuring cup and bowl. Assign each student a task: one to mea- sure the flour, another the salt, and another the water. All should take turns kneading. Test the consistency of each batch yourself and add flour or water if needed. Divide the clay and have the students store it in their plastic bags.

Start each class with a fairly structured pro- ject but leave plenty of time for the students to experiment on their own. Give each student a piece of aluminum foil (the size of their box lid) to work on. When they have finished, care- fully transfer the foil with the project and the baking instructions to the lid so that they can take their treasures home to bake. This will free your own oven for less fun things like dinner!

A baker's-clay project is usually done in two sessions—the first for forming and baking, the second for painting. The two can be com- bined if you dye the clay. Colored clay is more exciting for children, and it gives them the experience of combining color and form. It is also far less expensive than supplying a group with paints and brushes. Students 8 years old and up can help with the dyeing.

Mix the dye with the clay ingredients be- fore combining—this eliminates a lot of knead- ing and mess. To dye the clay, you will need the group equipment listed above plus:

1. nontoxic dye—dry or liquid tempera or paste food coloring
2. clear-plastic bags (at least 11″ × 13″)— two for each batch of clay

3. twist ties (the kind that come with plastic bags)
4. workshirts

For a medium color value add one of the following per batch:
1. ½ cup dry tempera to the flour and salt; or
2. ¾ cup liquid tempera to the water; or
3. 1 teaspoon paste food coloring to the water (be sure that the paste is dissolved in the water)

Your job as the teacher is to combine the flour and salt in a plastic bag (if you are dyeing with dry tempera, add and mix with the dry ingredients); add the water (if you are using food coloring or liquid tempera, combine with the water); seal the bag with a twist tie (get as much air out of the bag as you can); and place inside a second plastic bag. Each group of students should take turns kneading (about 8 minutes in all) and turn the clay out on a floured work surface, discarding the sticky inside bag. At this point you should check the consistency of each batch and add more flour or water if necessary. Have the students knead 2 more minutes on the floured surface. Divide the batches so that each student gets some of every color. Have the students store their clay in their own plastic bag.

Figures 8-1, 8-2, 8-3, and 8-4 show a fifth-grade project. The teachers asked the students to design a contemporary American flag. Plywood bases (the size of the school's ovens) were provided. The students were divided into four groups of eight. Each group was given two batches of each color—there was a lot of trading. After the flags were formed, they were baked 10 minutes at 200° and air-dried. After several weeks the flags were coated with polyurethane.

8-1. *American Flag* (18″ × 24″), a dyed-clay group project. (Courtesy of Madalena's group, Captain Wilkes fifth-grade class, Eileen Okada, Olga Ruys, and Ethie Williamson, teachers. Photo by Garnie Quitslund.)

8-2. *American Flag* (18″ × 24″), a dyed-clay group project. (Courtesy of Edith's group, Captain Wilkes fifth-grade class. Photo by Garnie Quitslund.)

8-3. *American Flag* (16″ × 24″), a dyed-clay group project. (Courtesy of Roby's group, Captain Wilkes fifth-grade class. Photo by Garnie Quitslund.)

8-4. *American Flag* (24" × 36"), a dyed-clay group project.
(Courtesy of David's group, Captain Wilkes fifth-grade
class. Photo by Garnie Quitslund.)

Index

aluminum foil 13, 16, 20, 22, 50, 55, 56, 57, 58, 61, 62, 72, 73, 83, 90

bag(s) *see* plastic, bag(s)
baker's clay
  for children 7, 10, 36, 80, 86, 90–93
  decoration of 80–87
    baked 85–87
    unbaked 83–84
  history of 9–10
  ingredients of 11–12
  mix(es)
    claylike 11, 12
    doughlike 11, 12
    materials 11
    methods 12
  preserving 88–89
  storage of 62
  teaching 10, 90–93
    materials 90, 91
    methods 90, 91
baking 11, 12, 13, 16, 18, 20, 22, 23, 24, 32, 34, 36, 48, 49, 50, 52, 60, 64, 65, 72, 73, 74, 76, 77, 78, 80, 81, 83, 85, 86, 87, 88, 90, 91
  sheet *see* sheet(s), cookie
  temperature(s) 12, 16, 20, 23, 24, 32, 36, 48, 50, 64, 73, 74, 81, 83, 91
  time(s) 12, 16, 20, 23, 50, 64, 73, 91
ball(s) 34, 35, 44, 46, 74, 83
  method(s) 34
base(s) 23, 24, 48, 50, 52, 62, 68, 69, 70, 72, 74, 76, 77, 91
basket(s) 55, 59, 60, 61, 62
bowl(s) 55, 59, 60, 61, 62, 64, 90
brace(s) 74, 76
braid(s) and braiding 11, 62, 64, 67
bread 7, 9–10
  ginger- 9, 13, 15, 16
breakage 88, 89
brush(es) 81, 88, 90
  glue 72

candleholder(s) 55, 57
candy, crushed 85, 86, 87
ceramic clay 11, 80, 83
children *see* baker's clay, for children
clock(s) 68
coating(s), protective 11, 41, 64, 73, 74, 80, 86, 88, 91
  finishes 88
coil(s) and coiling 11, 22, 34, 35, 42, 43, 44, 45, 46, 55, 60, 61, 62, 64, 74
  methods 35
color(s) and coloring 13, 23, 24, 26, 27, 36, 38, 56, 80–81, 85–87, 88
  crayon(s) 81
  flour(s) 22, 80
  food 26, 80, 81, 90, 91
  liquid 12, 80
  pen(s) 14, 80, 81
  with spice(s) 80
  value(s) 80, 91
see also dye(s) and dyeing; glaze(s) and glazing; paint(s) and painting; stain(s) and staining; tint(s) and tinting
cup(s), measuring 90
cutout(s) 12, 13–33, 66
  cookie-cutter 13, 14, 15–17, 20, 21, 25, 68
  freehand 13, 21–22, 30
  freestanding 16, 17
  materials 13
  methods 16, 20, 23, 24, 26–27
  pattern 13, 18–20, 21
  variations 23–33
cutting 11, 16, 20, 21, 23, 24, 28, 43, 62, 63, 66, 90

decoration(s) 9–10, 68, 80–87
  on baked clay 85–87
  frostinglike 8, 16, 84, 86
  on unbaked clay 82, 83–84
découpage 48, 80, 85

design(s) *see* figure(s); shape(s) and shaping
disk(s) 34, 35, 36, 43, 55, 83
  methods 35
dough 9, 10, 11, 46
  baked 83
  raw 11, 18, 20, 48, 52, 70, 78, 79
draping 20, 22, 55, 57, 62
drying 12, 44, 88, 91
dye(s) and dyeing 26, 39, 40, 68, 75, 80-81, 86, 87, 90, 91, 92, 93
  materials 90-91

fabric(s) 12, 18, 53, 60, 80, 85
fiberboard 76, 79
figure(s)
  animal 9, 10, 14, 18, 19, 21, 31, 33, 37, 42, 43, 48, 50, 51, 52, 53, 76
  bird 9, 10, 15, 21, 31
  cutout *see* cutout(s)
  Ecuadorian 8, 10, 16
  formed *see* shape(s) and shaping, formed
  geometric 9, 16, 27
  human 13, 14, 15, 16, 17, 18, 20, 22, 32, 36, 38, 39, 40, 44-46, 47, 48, 49, 50, 51, 58, 69, 70, 73, 76, 78, 89
  insect 25, 87
  movable *see* section(s), movable; shape(s) and shaping, movable
fishline 72, 73
flattening *see* shape(s) and shaping, flat
flour(s) 9, 11, 12, 13, 16, 22, 28, 32, 35, 58, 62, 90, 91
  cereal 80
  whole-wheat 28, 56, 80
folding 24, 25, 26, 27, 62
food coloring *see* color(s) and coloring, food
forming shape(s) *see* shape(s) and shaping, formed
frame(s) 15, 16, 26, 27, 41, 49, 65-75, 84
  materials 74
  methods 74
freestanding shape(s) *see* shape(s) and shaping, freestanding
frosting *see* decoration(s), frostinglike

garlic press *see* press(es) and pressing, garlic
gingerbread *see* bread, ginger-
glass 65, 69, 74, 83
glaze(s) and glazing, 64, 67, 70, 80-81, 88
  methods 81
  natural 80, 81
glue(s) 16, 50, 65, 72, 74, 78, 79, 85, 86, 88, 89
  brush *see* brush(es), glue
glycerine 11, 62
grommet(s) 72, 79

hairpin(s) 13, 16, 46, 90
hanger(s) 16, 18, 20, 23, 24, 32, 34, 36, 46, 72, 73, 88
hole(s) 11, 16, 20, 62
house(s) 69, 77

imprinting 11, 13, 23, 28, 29, 32, 33, 72

kneading 12, 13, 80, 90, 91
knives 13, 20, 23, 32, 34, 45, 62, 72, 85, 90
  electric 24
  paring 13
knot(s) 18

lamp(s) 62-64
large shape(s) *see* shape(s) and shaping, large
layering 13, 23, 24, 25, 26, 27, 36, 70, 79, 83
  methods 24

mask(s) 56, 57, 83, 85
materials
  baker's-clay mixes 11
  cutouts 13
  dyeing 90-91
  forming 34
  frames 74
  glazing 81
  plaques 72
  shaping 34, 62
  three-dimensional shapes 62
  teaching 90-91
metal 28, 65, 83
methods
  baker's-clay mixes 12
  balls 34
  coils 35
  disks 35
  flattening 36
  forming 34-35
  frames 74
  glazing 81
  large shapes 78-79
  layering 24
  painting 91
  plaques 72-73
  preserving 88
  rolling 12
  rounded shapes 44-46
  shaping 36, 44-46, 62-64, 78-79
  stripping 23
  teaching 90-91
  three-dimensional shapes 62-64
modeling paste 86
moisture 11, 16, 23, 24, 36, 45, 46, 64, 80, 86, 88
mold(s) and molding 9, 11, 32, 33, 55, 57
mount(s) and mounting 72, 74

nail(s) 74
napkin ring(s) 42

object(s) *see* figure(s); shape(s) and shaping
oilcloth 76, 79
ornament(s) 15, 44, 48
see also decoration(s)
oven(s) 7, 11, 12, 36, 48, 64, 65, 76, 81, 83, 91
  shapes larger than 76-79
see also baking
overlapping 13

paint(s) and painting 46, 50, 70, 73, 74, 80, 85, 86, 88, 90
  acrylic 86, 88
  enamel 86
  methods 91
  oil 86, 88
  tempera 80, 81, 88, 90, 91
  watercolor 86, 88
paper 18, 20, 80, 85, 90
  shelf 72
  transfer 72
  waxed 12, 23, 34, 44, 86
pasta 47, 83
pastry
  sheet *see* sheet(s), pastry
  tube 84, 86
pattern(s) *see* cutout(s), pattern; figure(s); shape(s) and shaping
pencil(s) 72, 73, 85
pinching 11, 34, 62
plaque(s) 22, 40, 48, 65–75, 91, 92, 93
  materials 72
  methods 72–73
plastic 65, 83
  bag(s) 62, 86, 90, 91
  drop cloth 90
plate(s) 54, 55, 56, 57, 58
plywood *see* wood, ply-
polyurethane 64, 86, 88, 91
see also coating(s), protective
potato ricer 28, 90
press(es) and pressing 11, 16, 20, 28, 32, 72
  garlic 11, 28, 34, 46, 78, 90
pretzel(s) 62, 63
project(s) *see* figure(s); shape(s) and shaping
protective coating(s) *see* coating(s), protective

rolling 11, 12, 13, 21, 23, 24, 26, 27, 28, 32, 34, 35, 38, 43, 44, 45, 46, 55, 56, 57, 62, 72, 73, 79, 90
  methods 12
  pin 12, 13, 24, 28, 32, 34, 62, 72, 90
rounded shape(s) *see* shape(s) and shaping, rounded
ruler(s) 23

salt 11, 12, 86, 88, 90, 91
sanding 66, 72
saw(s) and sawing, 66, 72
scissors 34, 45, 90
screw eye 72, 73
sculpture(s) 50–54, 76
section(s) 24, 38, 45, 52, 76, 79, 88
  movable 18, 19, 20, 76
sewing 53
shape(s) and shaping 9, 11, 12, 13, 16, 18, 20, 27, 32, 34–53, 69, 80
  flat 11, 13, 16, 36–43, 44, 60
    methods 36
  formed 12, 34–53, 55, 56, 57, 58, 63, 64, 65, 73, 76, 78, 83, 90

    materials 34
    methods 34–35
  freestanding 16, 18, 20
  in-the-round 50–54
  large 55–79
    methods 78–79
  larger than oven 76–79
  materials 34, 62
  methods 36, 44–46, 62–64, 78–79
  movable 18, 20
  rounded 44–49
    methods 44–46
  three-dimensional 55–64
    materials 62
    methods 62–64
  see also ball(s); coil(s) and coiling; cutout(s); disk(s); figure(s); pretzel(s); sculpture(s); strip(s) and stripping; twist(s) and twisting
sheets(s)
  cookie 12, 13, 16, 20, 23, 24, 27, 34, 62, 72, 73, 83, 86, 90
  pastry 12, 13, 34, 44, 62, 72
shellac 41, 88
see also coating(s), protective
spice(s) *see* color(s) and coloring, with spices
sponge 72
squeezing *see* press(es) and pressing
stain(s) and staining 74, 80, 86
stamping *see* imprinting
strip(s) and stripping 23, 24, 55, 61, 73, 74, 76, 79
  methods 23

tape 78
teaching *see* baker's clay, teaching
texture 13, 23, 28, 29, 30, 31, 36, 56, 80
three-dimensional shape(s) *see* shape(s) and shaping, three-dimensional
tint(s) and tinting 26, 64, 80–81
toothpick(s) 34, 40
turpentine 86
twist(s) and twisting 13, 62, 63, 64
  tie(s) 91

value(s) *see* color(s) and coloring, value(s)

wall hanging(s) 36, 37
water 11, 12, 13, 16, 34, 62, 81, 86, 88, 90, 91
waxed paper *see* paper, waxed
wire(s) 13, 16, 20, 34, 40, 46, 65, 76, 78, 83, 90
  electrical 62, 64
wood 65, 69, 72, 74, 76, 79, 83
  ply- 65, 66, 68, 70, 72, 74, 77, 91
wreath(s) 14, 43

yeast 9